I0098889

Stranger In

Christ

By

Setrol S Edmondson

Page Intentionally Left Blank.

Copyrights

Title: *Stranger in Christ*

Author: *Setrol S Edmondson*

Case Number: 1-14940254147

Copyright © 2025 Setrol Edmondson

All rights reserved.

No part of this publication may be reproduced or transmitted in any form or by any means without prior written permission from the author, except for brief quotations used in reviews or educational settings.

This is a work of Christian non-fiction based on the author's personal experiences and reflections. Some names or details may have been changed to protect privacy. The views expressed are individual and not intended as professional or doctrinal advice.

First Edition, 2025

Contact: setrol97@gmail.com

Dedication

This book is dedicated to my family, for whom I have received a prophecy that God will use me to bring them to **Christ**.

Acknowledgement

I would like to thank God the Father, the Lord Jesus Christ, and the Holy Ghost for giving me the visions that They gave me so that I can write about them. They gave me the fellowship of being a believer by granting me salvation and the inspiration of being an author to reach out to those who are in darkness to tell them about the magnificent light of the Word of God.

I thank my parents for birthing me and for the life they provided. My dad was my mentor growing up, and my mother encouraged me to write this book. In my sickness, where I was diagnosed with various mental illnesses, my family has played an integral role in being my support team by being columns in my life.

I thank my brethren Clive, who is an elder in the Lord, who told me to read the book From Babylon to Timbuktu. From the time I read that book, the Lord started to move in my life more than before. Missionary (Mervis Sewell) covered me in prayer and encouraged me to stay in the Word when the adversary attacked my mind and used the prayer line to develop my prayer life and endurance in the Lord. My cousin Tanya and her mother Maxine prayed for me late at night when I was going through spiritual warfare and couldn't sleep. I could call them at any hour during the night, and they covered me in prayer. I will always remember Camile, who was beside me when I saw the first vision in 2017, which was a vision of God Himself.

Table of Contents

Introduction 1

Childhood 3

2014 5

Lovelife 7

Near-Death Experiences 9

Visions 11

Fruit of the Spirit 14

Break 16

High School 18

2022 22

Spiritual Meltdown 25

Best Friends 27

Severe Affliction 30

Pastor Whitney 33

Test 37

Headback on the Bible 40

Kiss 42

Create in Me a Clean Heart 44

Prayer Line 48

Granddad 50

Grandmother 52

Living in Unbelief 54

People's Choice Carpet Cleaning 57

Yaad Spice 60

Mondson Trucking 62

Gnashing of Teeth 67

Wicked Spirits Raping Me in My Sleep 71

Wicked Spirits Tempting Me 74

Witches and Wizards in the Workplace 76

Meditation 79

Wisdom Entering My Heart 82

Dreams About People's Deaths 84

My Addiction to Porn 86

Fasting and Prayer 88

Jobs 93

How to Eat 96

Improved Health 98

Cleanliness 100

War 102

Conclusion 104

Introduction

I grew up in a traditional home with a father and a mother. They weren't my biological parents; instead, they were my grandparents. My mother lived on the other end of the island of Jamaica, and my dad lived in the United States. My aunt Lisa was like a mother to me and helped raise me before she moved to the U.S.

I grew up with some of my first and second cousins, and I had a blast growing up. My dad wanted the best for his children, so he sent my sister and me to a private school. My grandparents instilled love in us and never refrained from telling us how much our dad loved us and how he would give us the whole world if he could. He would often send money on our birthdays so we could celebrate with a party. Any time our school had a trip; he made sure we were able to attend.

I loved him, even though I didn't remember him as a little boy, because he had left Jamaica in pursuit of a better life. During summer holidays, when school was out, my sister and I would visit our mother in Hanover. I had an amazing childhood in Jamaica—but that all changed when I came to the United States.

Childhood

When I was in prep school, I used to dream that the most beautiful women in the world were my girlfriends. I was told that as a baby, I would place my hands inside women's shirts to feel their breasts for comfort. I would dance on my aunt's friends whenever they came by to visit.

One day at a football match, I approached a big woman and told her I liked her. She replied, "Hey likkle bwoy, mi and yuh anuh size." I was really drawn to big women growing up.

In grade four, I was called "dunce" by my teacher because I couldn't read Patois. In grade five, I joined the quiz team at St. Thomas Prep School. I played a match and did so well that the principal started calling me "Professor" because I used to teach the class. She adored me so much that she even wanted me to come live with her.

2014

From childhood, I had recurring dreams about the end of the world. I would be on the ground, watching people rise into the air toward Christ. In other dreams, people were ascending toward Him—but not me. These dreams terrified me, especially when I heard about the **mark of the beast** and the end times. Growing up in America, I believed I wouldn't die but would live to see Christ's return.

In 2014, the year I graduated from high school, I remember the clouds looking like they were getting closer to the earth. I didn't plan to continue my education, but my aunt Lisa told me I wasn't ready for the real world, and my dad encouraged me to return to school. That summer, I went to Jamaica to unwind and celebrate graduating from high school.

My dad's partner, Nicole, was upset that I went to Jamaica for the summer instead of going to summer classes at the university I had been accepted to. She told me that I had to run away when I reached the age of 17. I'm 28 now, and she was the one who actually put me out of the house. My dad had considered it before, but she had stopped him.

When I ran my dad's carpet cleaning business, I joined a round robin and received $2,000. I asked my step mom to hold it for me, but when I later requested it, she said she'd used it to pay for some classes. She once slapped me in the face for putting a whole carrot in the juicer, causing it to stop. Her mother once threw a slipper that hit my phone and broke it apart while I was listening to dancehall music. She said I was listening to "buggu-yaga music."

They acted as though their family was superior to ours, even though my dad's business was the main source of income supporting the household. He bought two carpet-cleaning vans. I would go with him to clean strip clubs, cars, restaurants, houses, and businesses. I've been working for as long as I can remember. That part of my life is hard to revisit—it was a time when I was drowning in depression and spiritual darkness.

Lovelife

I met Tashoy in 2014 after graduating high school in Jamaica. We started talking after she came overseas to visit one of my older cousins, Aunty Olive. I kissed her, and from that moment, something changed inside me. I loved her.

In 2015, she came to Orlando to visit Disney World. I saw her on my birthday. When I left Orlando, she cried—she didn't want to leave me. Years later, I married her.

We separated in 2022. Around that time, I started to like this new girl. The Holy Spirit told me that she was my wife. A pastor in Bull Bay prophesied that my wife would be a nurse and warned me not to choose anyone who was in darkness. She also said I had an executive anointing over my life.

Another pastor in Trinityville prophesied that God would bless Tashoy and me with a child soon, but said our relationship was full of trust issues and that I would have to initiate any reconciliation.

On the way to a fasting service, I was driving Tashoy's car— when the tire picked up a nail. At the service, the pastor prophesied that someone was facing hindrance. He called up Tashoy, asked if she had a boyfriend, and she said yes. He asked where he was, and she pointed to me in the church. The pastor prayed for both of our sex organs and told me that I needed to talk more or I'd find myself somewhere I didn't want to be if I didn't listen to the voice of God.

Near-Death Experiences

I had three near-death experiences in the summer of 2017. One morning on my way to school, I drove over a piece of cardboard on I-95. Something told me to stop and check under the car, but I ignored it. I was playing loud music and focused on a test I had that morning. A driver beside me tried to get my attention, and I read their lips—they were telling me my car was on fire.

I pulled over immediately. A car stopped in front of me and another behind me. One of them was an off-duty police officer. We looked under the car and saw the cardboard had caught fire. I used a baseball bat from my trunk to dislodge it and poured Gatorade on it to put the fire out. I thanked the good Samaritans who pulled over to assist me that morning. I made it to school, took my test, and passed. Thank God.

Another time, I was driving on the Turnpike when it started to drizzle. A man began drifting into my lane, and when I hit the brakes, my car began to swerve. It spun around three times and ended up on the soft shoulder. I was shaken but unharmed, and the car wasn't damaged. I continued to school that morning in shock and fear.

The third incident during that time occurred while I was traveling in the fast lane—the left lane—when I saw bright lights coming toward me. I quickly pulled into the middle lane, and a car sped past me going in the opposite direction. I was terrified because my life could've ended that night if I hadn't been paying attention to the road.

Visions

When I was in darkness, I saw the light, and it gave me hope. I don't remember the exact scenario, but it changed me. One morning, I was lying in bed and heard the door open. I thought it was my stepsister waking my brothers for school, but I couldn't move or speak—only look. A being entered the room. Its presence was holy. At the time, I wasn't walking with Christ, but I believe the being was an angel. It came to the head of the bed to do something to my head, then left. I thought of Jacob wrestling the angel on his journey, and I wanted to do that, but I couldn't move.

In May 2017, I picked up my mother-in-law from work and was at a stoplight when I saw a spirit before me. It was golden like the sun. I saw it from the chest down to its feet. Underneath its feet was brightness and glory. I didn't realize what I had seen until days later. I told my mother-in-law I had seen God. She said something in her spirit had told her to come to America that day. That was when I began to believe in the Christian God, despite the wickedness I had seen in the church.

I also saw the city of God in the sky one day while driving on I-95. It appeared bright, colorful, and magnificent—like a rainbow. Part of me wanted to pull over and stare, while another part feared to look upon it because of its purity. Another vision showed a figure standing in the sun, partially hidden by clouds. I saw his shadow cast on the earth, and the Holy Spirit told me it was Jesus Christ.

Another time, I saw thick gray clouds with silver linings overhead. Small black dots rose from the ground and were sucked into the clouds. The closest thing I can compare this vision to is when a magnet pulls objects toward it. I witnessed this vision two days in a row. The Holy Spirit told me that these last two were visions of the first and second resurrection.

Another day, I had a vision while driving back from Miami to West Palm Beach after visiting FIU with Ann, my dad's tax lady. I had just cried my eyes out, upset at how my dad's financial situation was affecting my education. When I arrived at the shop where he was, I handed him some papers to sign. Nicole's mother was there, and my dad asked, "You don't see your grandmother?" I greeted her, but inside I felt a fire in my eyes toward her. It was like I erased her from my heart, and though it all happened quickly, I couldn't move—I was frozen by the power of the Holy Ghost.

Outside, it started raining, and dark clouds came down and surrounded me. I went to work that night feeling completely drained by the energy I used when I felt that fire in my eyes. I didn't know a man could feel such power within himself—like having eyes of fire, like Christ. From that day, I knew not to go around certain people because of the hate and wickedness they directed toward me and my siblings when we were younger. They had slandered my family for years. My spirit was deeply vexed by them.

That night, lightning flashed intensely at work, and the residents encouraged me to think positively because they knew I had "connections." They could sense something divine was at work in me, though I had never told them about my visions. Some even asked me to read their minds—another gift God had blessed me with.

Fruit of the Spirit

I have experienced the joy of the Lord. He said He leaves His joy with us—not as the world gives, but a joy that no one can take away. But the devil used those closest to me to steal that joy. The Spirit brought back childhood memories, and my face glowed with the joy I felt.

I've also felt the peace of God—the peace that surpasses all understanding. It felt like heavenly waters were pouring into my soul for an entire day. I've only experienced the love of God once in full as a fruit of the Spirit, and that was while I was in Georgia. My entire being was encapsulated in love, and it felt like hatred no longer made sense.

The fruit of the Spirit is so pleasant and holy. I desire it more than anything else on earth. The enlightenment of the Spirit is sacred—it's the teacher mode of the Holy Spirit. I was scared at first when I experienced it due to the overwhelming brightness of His glory. One night, I became illuminated, and I've since repented for being afraid. I now desire to be taught by Him daily. I've grown to love, trust, and depend on Him. Though some things He does still make me tremble, I know now that He loves me and that He has no plans to harm me.

After all, He is the one healing me from everything I've suffered for Christ's sake.

Break

I took a break from reading the Word daily for about a year because I thought I was condemned. I had taken communion while experiencing severe homosexual thoughts, hoping for an immediate change, I didn't expect the change that took place in my body but I didn't feel anything. I assumed the communion had condemned me and confided in Missionary, who assured me that the Lord doesn't work that way.

My mind wasn't being renewed like before. I lived in fear and confusion, not understanding what I was going through. Eventually, I realized I was facing spiritual warfare. I had to fight those feelings and thoughts with the Word of God. Months went by without connecting with the Word. I was wallowing in misery, longing for deliverance but unsure how to get there.

Stranger in Christ

I didn't start fasting regularly until my ex came to live with me. I couldn't have sex with her because the medication I was taking had killed my desire. At first, she tried to help, but when I couldn't perform, she grew angry after each failed encounter and, after a while, gave up on having sex with me. That created a wedge in our relationship and contributed to our separation.

It hurt me deeply how things unfolded in the marriage, but God is still healing me. The divorce process is underway. The Holy Ghost told me to start taking communion again and confirmed it by having the reverend I studied with teach an entire lesson on it. Eventually, I began taking communion—not with crackers and grape juice as I had before, but this time with bread and wine. Since then, God has continued working wonders in my life.

High School

In high school, I was the awkward, nerdy Jamaican kid. While my friends danced, played sports, and participated in after-school activities, I stayed at school as long as I could to avoid going home.

I didn't choose the medical field—it chose me. In ninth grade, I was placed in an anatomy and physiology course, and I fell in love with learning the proper terminology for body parts, their systems, and their functions. I excelled in the class, and they placed me in the program again the following year. I was also part of the engineering program, but my mother wanted me to pursue that instead of healthcare. In their view, children shouldn't have a say in their career paths and the aspirations that they have for their future.

Stranger in Christ

Despite that, I completed the healthcare program and graduated high school with four licenses: Certified Nursing Assistant (CNA), Certified Medical Administrative Assistant (CMAA), EKG Technician, and Emergency Medical Responder. I was proud of myself for achieving so much at such a young age.

However, during clinicals for the CNA program, I realized I didn't enjoy the nature of the job. I started community college unsure of what I wanted to do. My Step mom encouraged me to get a degree in Health Services Administration, since my dad had a business and I was also interested in the health field. I followed her suggestion and eventually earned a bachelor's degree in that field.

While in college, I came under heavy spiritual attack. I didn't yet understand the spiritual realm, so I wasn't prepared for it. One morning, I woke up and saw the vision of God and what I saw was still in my mind, but the enemy attacked me to make it seem like God was bowing down to me. It scared me deeply, causing me not to want to go outside because the weather was stormy throughout that period. Any mighty lightnings would strike, causing me to tremble, followed by thunders that sounded like bombs were dropping. My health declined, I stopped eating, and I started losing weight rapidly. I believed I was condemned. I became afraid of going outside because of the ungodly and blasphemous thoughts plaguing my mind.

I had a dream where I was burning in fire, surrounded by people screaming in pain. But I was silent, and the flames didn't hurt me. In another dream, I saw that I was going to move to Georgia, but Lsia was upset about it. I eventually moved out of her house and found my own place because she said I wasn't contributing enough, and because of that, my ex wasn't allowed to visit anymore, and I wanted to live with her at that time.

I was motivated by a desire to get married and build a life with a woman. That dream didn't unfold the way I planned—it ended in divorce. Later, the Holy Ghost revealed to me that dark forces had worked witchcraft against me after I posted a birthday message and photo of Tashoy, who was then my fiancée. A man commented that she was wicked and hadn't told him she had a boyfriend. From that moment, things began to fall apart.

She came to live with me in December 2020. Just a few days after arriving, she took my car and left the apartment because she had gone through my computer and found messages between me and someone, she thought I was in a relationship with. But that person was just a friend; I wasn't in any relationship with her.

I told her that while she had been living her life freely, I had to seek refuge in friends and even strangers during my time of affliction.

It wasn't always like this between us. In the past, she had helped me fight through spiritual warfare. Before I came to understand the spiritual realm, she would pray for me and encourage me in the Lord. I remember one time when she came overseas while I was being afflicted. We were lying in bed, and a wicked spirit struck her in the head right beside me, and she prayed away the spirit.

Two years ago, I asked the Holy Spirit if I could divorce her, and He told me no. I didn't understand why He wanted me to remain married to her—but now she's a U.S. citizen and serving in the Navy. Looking back, I'm grateful I obeyed the Spirit. At the very least, I won't be viewed as someone who brought her to the U.S. and then abandoned her.

This walk with Christ—it's truly an interesting one.

2022

This was the year I got separated from my wife. Nicole told her a lie — she claimed I said I was going to kill her. I never said anything like that. And truthfully, if I were going to do something like that, I wouldn't need Nicole's permission. But I didn't tell her such a wicked thing. I was at the Anchor ⚓ mental health facility at the time. That lie was the final blow to a relationship that was already breaking apart. After that, everything just fell apart completely.

The Lord tested me during that period and told me He was going to use me to start World War 3. While I was in the facility, Russia invaded Ukraine. My great-grandmother passed away during that time, and I didn't even get to attend her funeral.

The Lord also told me He would reveal some of His elect to me. One day, while I had my hand in the Bible, a spiritual sword began to form in my hand. I couldn't take my hand out of the Bible until it was finished. It shocked me. I had already received a prophecy that the Lord would give me a sword — one I would use to protect my family — but I never imagined it would manifest in such a literal and supernatural way.

My eyes burned during that experience, and I had to ask God for strength just to endure it. It made me realize how important I am to God, that He would choose me for such a task.

While in the facility, I met a man who said his name was "the devil." After he told me that, I viewed him as the enemy — and it made things worse because he was my roommate. I started praying Scripture over the room, and the person who had spiritual control over that being came into the facility, asking me to show mercy. But there's no such thing in the war of God — I had no pity.

A Jewish man came in early one morning and pleaded for mercy on the being's behalf. My psychiatrist was a man of Indian descent, and he kept prescribing me medications without much explanation. One day, God made him bow in front of me. He dropped his pen while standing next to me, and God showed me that he feared me.

After being released from the facility, God led me to work in a hospital setting. That experience inspired me to go back to school to become a nurse.

Spiritual Meltdown

I got involved with one of Marika's friends, and it turned out to be a complete nightmare. She wanted me to leave my girlfriend for her because she said I had my head on straight. One night, while we were having sex, the condom came off and I ejaculated inside her. I panicked, thinking she might get pregnant, so I bought her a Plan B pill. She told me she'd take it when she got home, but I insisted on seeing her take it, and she eventually did.

That night, after I got home and lay down, I felt a pressure come and sit on my head. Suddenly, I was plunged into a state of confusion. I lost my appetite, started losing weight, and my mental clarity was gone. Eventually, my parents brought me to a psychiatric hospital. I was there for three days, diagnosed with acute psychosis, and prescribed medication.

At the time, I was working at Yaad Spice as a cashier. One day, a woman came in, cussing and shouting that she always got the wrong order and service was too slow. Other customers tried to calm her down and reminded her of customer service standards. But I broke down in tears. I couldn't even respond to the woman because of what I was going through spiritually. That day was my last at Yaad Spice.

When my dad asked me what happened, Nicole told him I couldn't handle pressure and shouldn't return to the restaurant. She even suggested he take me to an obeah man. But instead, he called a Christian woman named Missionary.

Missionary asked me what had happened, and I told her — including the sexual encounter. She spoke in tongues and had my dad anoint my head with olive oil. I felt a shift in my head right then. She told me I had to be careful of the spirits I encounter because I am a child of God.

But I remember thinking to myself: *How can I be a child of God when I don't even believe in the Christian God?*

Best Friends

I have two best friends — one is a man, and the other is a woman. Sanny and I grew up together in Jamaica, and we both moved to the States around the same time. We've had a close relationship since our youth, and even now, we can talk about anything for hours.

During my time of affliction, it felt like I had no one to talk to, like I was going through everything alone. But now that God is bringing me out of it, and Sanny and I have started talking regularly again, I realize I wasn't truly alone after all. In fact, he was the one who gave me the title for this book: *Stranger in Christ* — and the Spirit told me to keep it.

Shanice and I met in community college, and we've been friends ever since. We would call each other, check in, and we would even play games while talking on the phone. I used to read her the mix-up posts from the *Dear Dream* page on

Instagram, and we'd laugh and chat about them. We talked about God and sang hymns together — mostly in the summer when she had time off from work, because she's a teacher.

She always told me I love to work and reminded me to remember her when I get rich. Whenever I was sick, she'd know because she wouldn't hear from me, and the next time we talked, she'd ask, "Were you in the mad house again?" When I got my apartment, she bought me my TV. She also filed for her mother to come live with her, and her mom always asked for me.

Blanca and I grew up together in Spring Garden — we were neighbors. I later found out he was living in Palm Beach, and we reconnected. We shared stories about childhood and adulthood. He served in the U.S. Marines and told me about his experiences. We also talked about the Bible and the work of the Most High in his life. He told me he was leaning toward the Muslim faith, but also said I was the closest thing he's ever seen to Jesus.

I met a girl on a plane when I was returning to the States after taking my little brother to Jamaica because he wasn't behaving himself. We sat next to each other, and I started a conversation, then asked for her number. We talked as friends at first, but didn't enter a relationship until more than a year later — after the Spirit told me she would be my wife.

She met me at the most downtrodden point in my life. I was hurting deeply from what my ex had done to me, and yet she still gave me a chance. I didn't tell her I was married until after we got involved. I never meant to deceive her. I had already told her I was going to marry her because I was being obedient to the Spirit. Now I'm following through with that promise, as the divorce process is already underway.

Right now, she's my favorite person. She's soft, gentle, loving — and everything about her is wife like. But I'm waiting on the instruction of the Holy Ghost before doing anything, because *obedience is better than sacrifice.*

My cousin Kimola calls me her favorite cousin and lovingly refers to me as "Fireball." Chunny has always encouraged me to become a minister of the gospel because she sees the passion I have for it. Jake has been my favorite cousin since childhood. When I was in Jamaica last year and fell sick, he cared for me like a brother.

Severe Affliction

During my time of deep distress and affliction, I went to a church where many people were speaking in tongues at the same time. To me, it sounded like confusion. A prophet was present and called up people to give them prophecies about their lives.

I asked my cousin to come with me, so we were there together. The Spirit gave my cousin a word, and I was offended — because I had come seeking a word for my life, and he got one and I didn't. But I didn't understand how the Spirit worked back then. I was just desperate for comfort in the midst of my suffering.

Still, I didn't leave without consolation. That prophet gave me a word that has since come to pass. He told me that the Lord was going to give me a sword that I would use to protect my family. I don't remember everything else he said, but that part stayed with me vividly. After that experience, homosexual thoughts began to bombard my mind. I wanted to escape them by any means necessary.

Later, I met a prophet named Asare. The story of how I met him is quite interesting — he was the one who had previously given a prophecy to Tashoy about her future husband.

When I met him, he asked me, "Why are you seeking an ex-wife all the way in Jamaica?" He told me God wanted to make a covenant with me, and that I needed to pay tithes because that was the law of God. He said I should give a tenth of what I earned — and even add something extra for him.

I brought my little brother and his mother to his church. He told me I needed to take communion, but his version of communion was having me bathe in grape juice for seven days — without any bread or wine to represent the body of Christ. It was just the "blood," and honestly, it felt like an unholy ritual.

I paid tithes for a while, but when I stopped due to financial strain, he asked me why. I told him I didn't have any money, and he replied that he would revoke his angel's protection from over my life — basically revealing himself as a devil. I told my mother-in-law what he said, and she apologized for ever sending me to him.

Pastor Whitney

I once attended a church led by a white pastor who also had a younger associate pastor. I opened up to them about the issues plaguing my marriage. I wasn't having sex with my wife due to the side effects of the medication I was on — they had made me impotent and disconnected me from my spiritual intimacy with Christ. I was furious inside, because the person I used to be didn't have those problems.

The pastor advised me to pray separately from my wife. He said maybe there was an area of my life that God wasn't pleased with. Both he and the younger pastor prayed for us. While they prayed, I felt the breeze of the Holy Ghost — a peaceful confirmation that I wasn't alone. Before going to that church, I had visited another pastor in Palm Beach. I told him about the demonic thoughts I was experiencing, and instead of praying with me, he said I needed to see a psychiatrist. That upset me deeply. I had just shared with him how I'd seen God, how I'd experienced His goodness in my life, and how I was fighting against demonic attacks — and his solution was a referral to see the psychiatrist.

Later, I visited another white pastor who asked me if I liked music. I told him I did, and he said music would be part of my ministry. I think he also hinted that I'd be on TV one day. I do love music — it's been an anchor for me, especially when I've felt low. I use it to lift my spirit.

My mother once received a word from the Lord saying her son was going to receive a scholarship for school. Eventually, the Holy Spirit gave me clear instructions: I was to go back to school to become a nurse.

I got accepted into nursing school in Florida but later resigned due to a serious incident that happened in May. Still, the instructions from the Spirit remained: go back to school, get my BSN (Bachelor of Science in Nursing), then my Nurse Practitioner license, then move on to become a CRNA (Certified Registered Nurse Anesthetist), and finally, a Nurse Anesthesiologist. With God's help, I intend to walk that path.

Stranger in Christ

The Spirit also told me that God would bless me with more than one wife and not to worry about how I'd provide for them — He would make me exceedingly fruitful. He said I wouldn't have children here on earth, but He would bless me with seed in the kingdom.

One night, I had a dream where I was standing in a doorway with my hands raised over my head. On the bed, there was a woman and a baby. The woman pointed at me and said to the child, *"See daddy deh."*

Now the Spirit is revealing to me that I am a king before God and one of Christ's apostles. He told me I am of the seed of David and that He's going to build me a house.

Two years ago, I started wearing perfume, and one day, the Spirit of God kissed me on the lips and told me that men would worship me. It was so intimate that I was stunned. I told God I didn't want anyone worshipping me — but two years later, I've seen the truth in His words.

As a CNA, people often come up to me and say I'm the only one they want caring for them. Some call me their "nurse." Both patients and coworkers have told me I would make a great nurse — and even a doctor. The love I've been shown is Christlike.

I was accepted into South Florida State College for the LPN (Licensed Practical Nurse) program. I had applied to the RN program, but I didn't make it in — I missed it by a slim margin. Then two additional seats opened up in the LPN program, and I was offered one. I accepted it, partly because it was a requirement for staying at my aunt's house.

Before that, I had been accepted into a private university for my BSN and had already started school. I was so happy. But when I asked for time off work due to mental health challenges, the hospital insisted I return before the date I requested, so I resigned.

I haven't worked since August, and I'm grateful that God has given me this time to focus on my mental health — to love myself and to love Christ — so I can love His people and care for them from a healthier place.

I've seen job listings in Jamaica paying between 2 to 5 million JMD per year. That opened my eyes. I thought, *Wow, I can be back home, working comfortably while going back to school as the Holy Ghost instructed.*

Test

Before I was admitted to the Anchor ⚓ mental health facility, I had been fasting.

During that time, I asked God for permission to come off the fast so He could reveal my wive to me and show me some of His elect. He told me that He was going to use me to start World War 3.

He instructed me to drive around the FedEx parking lot at His command. Then He told me to drive — and as I drove, He began to speak to me. At one point, He told me to stop the van in the middle of the road and take out my Bible. He told me which scriptures to read and kept asking, "Are you ready?"

Then His tone changed — He began speaking in an angry voice. It shook me to the core. I thought He was going to kill me. The tone alone filled me with terror. He told me to repent — for my sins and for the sins of my wife. I kept repenting, over and over, as fast as I could, feeling like I was running out of time. My life flashed before my eyes. I thought that was the end.

Then a car hit my dad's van because it was parked in the middle of the road. I got out and sat in the other driver's vehicle — a woman's van. She was frightened and called the police. When they arrived, they evaluated me and took me to the hospital.

God told me to focus on His voice and not to listen to the staff. I didn't speak until my ex arrived at the hospital. After that, the staff conducted a psych evaluation. They asked if I had a history of mental health issues, and I told them about my diagnosis. They brought my ex outside the room and had a conference call with my family.

Eventually, the hospital decided to Baker Act me — a legal process to commit someone involuntarily for mental health evaluation. Afterward, my ex looked at me and asked, "Why are you ripping my heart out of my chest?" And I was just lying there on the bed, silent, thinking, *Really?*

Stranger in Christ

I spent three weeks in that facility. But God had a purpose for it — He sent me there to minister to the people inside. I witnessed fights, but no one touched me. God protected me.

A local Congress representative was contacted to investigate how the facility was being run because they were mistreating patients. They would tell us we were being discharged, only to change the date. The psychiatrist kept switching up my medication without explaining anything.

There were times they held me down and injected me because I refused treatment.

After I was finally discharged, Nicole told my dad and Tashoy that I wasn't better and tried to convince them to send me back to the facility. But I was already cooperating with the nurse practitioner, and she said I didn't exhibit the signs of someone with schizophrenia. She believed in me and wanted to work with me — but I ended up losing my insurance, and the treatment was discontinued.

Headback on the Bible

During the height of my affliction, there were weeks when I couldn't sleep. I'd lie in bed with my mind racing nonstop, knowing I still had to wake up and go to work. The thoughts that tormented me the most were the homosexual ones — they were the strongest and most persistent.

No matter where I turned for comfort, the torment followed me. I tried watching movies, hoping they would ease my mind, but then even the movies would start to take on a life of their own — as if they were being twisted to disturb my spirit.

My ex had these eyes — ornaments or trinkets — that she would leave around the house, and the adversary tempted me to put them on. I tried distracting myself with TikTok, but even that became a source of torment, filled with temptations that only fed the battle going on in my mind.

Then the Holy Spirit showed me something simple but powerful: I could use the Bible as a pillow. That simple act brought me peace. On the nights when I couldn't read anymore, I would rest my head on the closed Bible or even lay it open beneath me — and that alone brought me sleep.

I was so afflicted that the pages of my Bible began turning yellow from the discharge coming out of my head. But looking at where I've come from, I know I'm in a much better place today — even though I'm not fully healed yet.

I've had many prayer warriors pray for me over the years. Now, I finally understand why certain things happen in church and in the lives of believers. The afflictions and temptations of the adversary are real. He doesn't want to go into the lake of fire alone, so he tries to drag us down with him.

One day while I was driving, my family saw me with the Bible behind my head. They called me crazy. My dad asked me, "Who did you ever see doing things like that?" I told him, "Nobody." Because it wasn't about following someone else — it was what the Holy Spirit had revealed to me for my healing.

Kiss

After I got separated from Tashoy, I started treating myself better. I began wearing perfumes, going to the movies, and buying myself ice cream. I was learning to take care of me — to enjoy life again, even in small ways.

One day, while I was in that season of healing, the Spirit of God kissed me on the lips. I was completely taken aback. Then He said to me, "People are going to worship you." I immediately responded, "I don't want anyone worshiping me."

That moment reminded me of *Psalm 2:12*:

"Kiss the Son, lest he be angry, and ye perish from the way, when his wrath is kindled but a little. Blessed are all they that put their trust in Him."

Stranger in Christ

When Tashoy's mother was heading back to Jamaica, I brought her to the airport. She kissed me on my cheek and hugged me before leaving. That moment stood out too — like a bookend to the chapter that was closing in my life.

Create in Me a Clean Heart

When I got sick this time around, it was at the end of 2019, right before COVID came around. I received a word from one of God's ministers that I was going to end up in a place I didn't want to be if I didn't listen to the voice of the Spirit. That word came to pass because I have been living in severe affliction ever since.

One morning, I woke up and my mind was telling me that I was Satan's disciple. I got scared and called Missionary to pray for me. I heard a voice that sounded like my dad's saying, "TJ, get up. TJ, get up." I got out of bed but received no further instructions. I was tired, so I laid back down—and that's when the affliction grew heavier. My mind was filled with nothing but wickedness. It felt like I had a double mind. One part was consumed by evil thoughts that wanted to take over my entire being.

Stranger in Christ

I had to start reading the Word more than I ever had before. I began to fast consistently. At one point, my mind even tried to convince me that I was a tare, and I had to fight to believe I was a wheat. I begged God to make me sensitive to sin again. My mind had wicked imaginations against Christ, and the enemy wanted me to commit abominable acts. These thoughts kept intensifying.

Even when I tried watching Christian movies to calm my mind, it was like my mind took on a life of its own—twisting everything, even inserting homosexual thoughts into scenes. I had no peace—day or night. I had to stay rooted in the Word of God constantly so that the fire of His truth could burn the wickedness out of my flesh.

The Spirit worked on my mind little by little. First, He burned away the corruption. Then He began to create in me a new mind. My heart had turned to stone, and the Word began to soften it—replacing it with a heart of flesh. I could tell He wasn't just working on my mind but on my entire body.

I was amazed at the care and intimacy God showed me during this process—and continues to show me. I learned that worshiping God is about intimacy with Him. When the Scripture says to *"work out your own salvation with fear and trembling"* (*Philippians 2:12*), I finally understood what that meant.

When David cried out in Psalm 51, *"Create in me a clean heart, O God; and renew a right spirit within me"* (*Psalm 51:10*), I realized that was exactly what was happening in my life. I was terrified to know that my mind had sinned against God, but He was right there, gently burning the rot out of me—never once despising my broken heart or contrite spirit.

He told me He loved me and reminded me to be careful at work. He encouraged me when I was low, depressed, or full of doubt. He even sang to me when I felt sad. He told me jokes to make me smile and brought back positive memories to keep me anchored when the pain from my spiritual "open heart surgery" was too much to bear.

I started doing Bible study with Tanya, and we would minister to each other. She was amazed at the knowledge and understanding of Scripture God had blessed me with. She told me that many pastors didn't have the kind of delivery I did and that she always learned something new when we studied together.

Stranger in Christ

As I stay in the Word and let the Father continue to heal and comfort me, I look forward to growing—from glory to glory, from faith to faith, to deeper depths and higher heights.

Prayer Line

I began joining the prayer line after I started coming under spiritual attacks. I would start my mornings by reading the Word, and later, I would join in prayer. At first, I was shy when praying because I was doing it in front of other people, and I was afraid I wouldn't say the right words. But over time, I grew more confident.

I received several prophecies from the prayer line. The members told me I was a chosen vessel and reminded me that they were covering me in prayer. One morning, I remember the prayer line had to be shut down because of the intense spiritual attack I was under. I asked them to cover me, but they also came under attack. That morning, I felt hopeless.

Missionary has called me both the prophet Jeremiah and the patriarch Joseph. She gave me a word that God was using me to bring my family to Christ—and now I can see that prophecy unfolding day by day.

Granddad

Traina used to tell me that I should go to school and focus on my lessons, because whatever the teacher teaches is for me alone—no one else can take that knowledge from my brain. He said that if I followed his advice, one day I'd be able to pick, choose, and refuse women. I took his words seriously, and now I see the truth in what he said.

Today, women are the ones pursuing me, and I don't even have to say a word. Their mothers, aunts, and grandmothers tell me that I would make a great husband for their daughters, nieces, or granddaughters—some of whom they proudly say are virgins. When I receive compliments like that, I feel honored, because I kept my granddad's teachings close to my heart.

Another one of his proverbs was, "The humblest calf sucks the most milk." In his later years, he said he wasn't sure if that saying still held true, but I reassured him that it did. Since I started walking with the Lord, I've seen that humility truly brings blessing.

Grandmother

My grandmother died a year after I moved to the States. She used to say that she knew her time was coming soon. When she was alive, she held my entire heart. I hadn't loved anyone with the depth that I loved her. I loved my ex deeply with a godly love, but if my grandmother had still been alive when I saw God, I believe I would have loved her even more.

Now, the person I love most in this world is the Lord Himself. I give myself to Him daily, for the purpose of His kingdom.

My grandmother saw God when I was still living in Jamaica, and she told me about it. I don't remember the exact story, but I remember two possibilities—or maybe it was both. Either one day it was raining, and after it stopped, the sun came out, and she saw God take the sun back into the clouds with His hands. Or she said that one day God stretched out His hand and then pulled it back into His bosom.

The Scriptures say the Lord afflicts us for our sins, but *"His hand is stretched out still"* (*Isaiah 5:25, Isaiah 9:12, Isaiah 9:17, Isaiah 9:21, Isaiah 10:4*), because He wants us to return to Him. The Holy Spirit brought that verse back to my remembrance after I had my own vision of God. It reminded me that I came from a deeply spiritual home, and the teachings of my grandparents have carried me through this life.

There's a proverb that says, *"Train up a child in the way he should go: and when he is old, he will not depart from it"* (*Proverbs 22:6*). That was true for me.

When I told my grandmother that I wanted to go back to Jamaica because I didn't like it in the U.S., she encouraged me to "bend my mind to my condition." Her words comforted me.

When she died, I didn't cry—but I felt it to my core. The pain lingered with me for years.

Living in Unbelief

Growing up in Jamaica, my prep school had devotions every morning. We prayed before lunch, after lunch, and again before we were dismissed for the day. At night, I would pray before going to bed, and I kept that habit when I moved to America.

In the U.S., school started each day with the Pledge of Allegiance. That was how the society marked the beginning of the school day. I got baptized at an early age in the Seventh-day Adventist Church. But after I was baptized, I stopped believing in God. I drifted away from the values I was raised with. Throughout my teenage years, I lived in spiritual darkness and depression, especially after I went to live with my dad. Before that, I had been living with my aunt Sherron—whose house I just recently left to return to Jamaica. During those years, I became fascinated with Greek mythology. I read books on the subject, and while reading them, my conscience tried to warn me, but I ignored it and kept going. It was a whole series, and after I finished it, I didn't continue reading mythology anymore.

Later on, as I began walking with the Lord and experiencing affliction from wicked spirits, I learned that reading those books was a sinful act. I repented and asked the Lord to forgive me. I didn't know it was a sin at the time—especially since those books are easily available to teenagers in libraries across high schools. Still, I felt ashamed, like I had betrayed God. But He took my guilt and shame away.

Even as I write this now, tears are coming to my eyes. I pray for strength—to endure temptation and not fall back, so I won't crucify the Son of God afresh. I'm grateful that God is merciful, and that He gave His only begotten Son, so that whoever believes in Him will not perish but have everlasting life.

There was a time when I said God wasn't real, and that I didn't believe in the Christian God because of the wickedness I saw in the church. I remember having a Bible but only opening it occasionally to read Proverbs. I could see the wisdom in its pages, but that was as far as I went.

Back then, I told myself I wanted to travel to Ethiopia and visit the churches carved into the rocks at Lalibela. I believed man had changed the Word of God, and I wanted to see where the original truth was preserved. The Bible says that anyone who adds to the Word will have the plagues written in it added to them, and anyone who takes away from it will have their part removed from the Book of Life.

But then, just like with the Apostle Paul, God gave me a life-changing encounter. I didn't need to travel to Ethiopia no more for that reason, but I would still like to go. God Himself revealed to me that He is real—and that His Word is my life source. Now, I dwell in it day and night, and I labor in it with all my heart.

People's Choice Carpet Cleaning

In high school, I used to go with my dad to help him clean carpets. He planned for me to take over the business after I graduated—and he followed through on that promise. When I finished school, he gave me the business.

I started working full-time, cleaning carpets while attending community college. But I wasn't making the kind of money my dad was making, and he assumed I was sending all my earnings to Tashoy in Jamaica. That couldn't have been further from the truth.

As time went on, I became sick, and going to work became a daily battle. Jobs that would normally take me thirty to forty-five minutes started taking two to three hours. I felt like

I was in a constant state of confusion. My mind was scattered, and my spirit was weighed down.

Eventually, I found the courage to tell my dad that I was going to shut down the business. He was angry about my decision and didn't speak to me for a while. He felt all his years of hard work had gone to waste, and that I hadn't even tried. He told me I was the weakest of his children—and those words cut deep.

Later, when I started experiencing spiritual attacks, he told me that God didn't like me. I wanted to ask him if God liked Jesus—because Jesus Himself said we must take up our cross and follow Him. The world persecuted Jesus, so it will persecute His followers too. The servant is not above his master.

Despite everything, I've had believers tell me how strong I am for enduring what I've gone through and still standing. A missionary told me that most people wouldn't have survived the things I've faced. Camile said the same. Even Tashoy— after we separated—told me she couldn't have endured what I went through.

Now, my sister Marika and other family members tell me that I'm strong. One of my dad's lady friends even told me I'm the strongest of his children.

Stranger in Christ

God used all the affliction I went through to strengthen me for His purpose. Now, I carry myself as one of God's chosen vessels—not in arrogance, but in humility.

Just yesterday, a friend of mine in Kenya told me I have a beautiful soul. She even said I was the most beautiful soul she's ever met. Another friend I grew up with once told me I'm the closest thing he's seen to Jesus Christ. When I worked at the hospital, some of my coworkers said I was Christlike.

I don't labor to be rich—I labor to be more like Christ.

Yaad Spice

Yaad Spice, the restaurant, opened while I was attending community college. At the time, I was juggling school and working at People's Choice Carpet Cleaning. I was excited that my dad was opening another business, so I helped out whenever I had free time.

I started off washing dishes, especially when the sink was full. As the restaurant picked up, I was taught how to serve the food. Eventually, I was doing both—washing dishes and serving meals. Since the business wasn't moving fast enough yet to hire a cashier, my dad asked me to operate the register. I did all of this in the beginning, helping to get the business off the ground.

Once things got busier, my dad and his business partner began hiring staff. I had been a valuable asset in launching the restaurant, but I was eventually let go after an incident involving a rude customer.

One day, a woman came into the restaurant cussing and complaining about how her order was always wrong and how long it took to get served. Other customers were trying to calm her down and speak kindly, but I couldn't respond. I was going through a lot spiritually, and I broke down crying.

That was my last day at Yaad Spice.

My dad asked me what happened, and Nicole said I couldn't handle pressure. She told him I shouldn't return to the restaurant because I was "bad for business."

I couldn't help but reflect on all the pressure I'd already endured—and survived. But suddenly, I was being told I couldn't handle stress. It hurt to be dismissed so easily, especially after all I had contributed.

Mondson Trucking

My dad's woman sold her house in Palm Beach and moved to Georgia. In her mind, my brother's mother was trying to take her house by using my sister Marika and my younger brothers. The wickedness she had done to me and my siblings was catching up to her, and my brothers eventually told their school about what she had done. As a result, she was being investigated. She believed my brother's mother was trying to move into the house with my dad.

Years passed, and rent in West Palm Beach became outrageously expensive. I couldn't find anywhere to live for less than $1,600 a month, and that didn't even include the first month's rent, last month's rent, and the security deposit. I was working at an assisted living facility at the time and had just received a job offer from the post office, but I had nowhere to stay. My lease was ending, and I couldn't renew it on my own because my housemate was moving away.

At that point, I was on speaking terms again with my dad's woman, and she encouraged me to move to Georgia. She said it was a good place for young people and that jobs were easy to find. I fasted and prayed about it, and the Spirit led me to go.

My ex didn't want to go live with Nicole. She wanted me to go first, find a place, and then she would join me. But Nicole convinced her to come with me. My dad also wanted me to move because he was starting a trucking business and wanted me to be a part of it.

I moved to Georgia with Tashoy and started working at FedEx, where Kedisha also worked, while handling paperwork for the new business. My dad wanted me to go on the road with him, driving the truck, but I told him I preferred to stay home and try to work on my marriage. I offered to be the dispatcher instead, calling brokers and securing loads for the truck. He had purchased a box truck from a young man in Florida to get started.

While staying at Nicole's house, I continued to fast and pray. The atmosphere in the home was hostile. My little sister, Sanesha, had already been living there, and Nicole—along with her daughter and her daughter's friends—would constantly pick on her.

My dad didn't believe I was doing enough to find loads for the truck, so he hired another dispatcher. The truth is, I was focused more on seeking healing and deliverance from God. I spent most of my time in the Word, praying, and fasting when I wasn't working.

I valued my spiritual well-being over everything else.

I knew I was spiritually sick, so I poured all of my energy into seeking the Lord—into healing the pain in my mind and body, and dealing with the scars left by infidelity and disrespect in my marriage. Because of my medical condition, I couldn't maintain an erection, and during my entire marriage to Tashoy, we were only able to have intercourse successfully once.

To make matters worse, after nearly a year of living together, she dismissed that one moment we shared by saying, "It wasn't even sex." I still don't fully understand what she meant, but those words cut deep. They haunted me.

All I could do was take my hurt to the Lord in prayer.

I felt stuck—like I was caught between a rock and a hard place. I wanted to end the marriage, but the Lord kept telling me not to. I didn't realize He was going to end it Himself. And now, two years later, we are in the process of getting divorced.

After I was discharged from Anchor Mental Hospital, I was kicked out of Nicole's house. She wanted my dad and Tashoy to call the police to force me back into the hospital because she claimed I wasn't "well." Neither of them did. I had plans to go to Jamaica, but I changed my mind. When I told her that, she said I couldn't stay in her house if I wasn't taking the medication. So, I packed my things and left.

Nicole later told Tashoy that I said I was going to kill her— a complete lie. I never said anything like that. But because of it, Tashoy became afraid of me.

I can't forgive Nicole—for working witchcraft against me, for sowing the seeds that destroyed my marriage, and most of all, for trying to destroy the new relationship God has now blessed me with.

When I returned to Jamaica, I didn't even go inside my dad's house. I don't want anything to do with her or anyone tied to her.

I even had a dream that I was lying in a bed, uncovered, with a Bible behind my head. In the dream, Nicole came into the room and tried to have sex with me. I woke up furious.

Gnashing of Teeth

My eyes would twitch, burn, and sometimes even run water. The Word says that if your right hand offends you, you should cut it off—for it's better to enter eternal life maimed than to have your whole body cast into the fire. I could hear my teeth gnashing against each other, and the bones in my face would make noise as the Spirit worked to heal my mind.

When my family saw my face moving and asked me why I was doing that, I told them it wasn't me—it was the Spirit of God healing me.

My spiritual bones had been broken and shattered. It felt like my skull was wide open, and the bones surrounding my brain were pressing in, almost like my brain was being punctured. It felt as if part of it was missing. My memory had significantly weakened, and my brain activity had slowed. I wasn't operating spiritually the way I had when I was first baptized by the Holy Ghost.

My mind wasn't being renewed like it used to be. After a fast, I didn't feel myself rising in the Spirit like I did when I first began fasting. Nothing felt the same anymore.

I remembered what it was like in the beginning when I had been enlightened. I thought I had lost that light. I became afraid—thinking I had fallen too far. A passage in the book of Hebrews haunted me. It says that it is impossible for those who were once enlightened, and who have tasted the heavenly gift and been made partakers of the Holy Ghost, to fall away and be renewed again—because they would be crucifying the Son of God afresh.

But now, I can confidently say: I am not condemned.

The Spirit of God still speaks to me daily. He is still binding up the wounds in my mind and body. It feels like He's performing open-heart and open-brain surgery on me. He is so gentle and so careful.

Because of the work, the time, and the patience that God has poured into healing me, I feel compelled to return to nursing school—and to be a great healthcare worker. I made a vow to the Lord that I would continue working hands-on with patients, standing on the floor to care for them, instead of sitting in a desk job in management.

As God heals me, I've become more aware of how the human body works, and how different foods and drinks affect its function. I no longer belong to myself. I've given myself fully to the work of Christ's kingdom.

When I was still with my ex and my eyes would twitch or my teeth would gnash, she suggested I get checked out. I didn't want to. But when I got into a car accident in Atlanta and was taken to the hospital, they ran every test—CT, CAT, MRI—and all came back normal. No physical injury. Nothing was wrong.

Still, my ex accused me of being in a cult. That hurt, because all I was doing was having Bible study with elders, using Scripture-based lessons. There was nothing cult-like about it.

It wasn't until certain words were said to me—and those words started replaying in my mind—that I realized just how much pain I had been carrying from the relationship. My only outlet became talking to God. People suggested therapy, but I declined. I saw God as my Wonderful Counselor.

I felt like the effort I was putting in to seek God wasn't being seen or appreciated. When I tried to express this, my ex said, "You don't know what I do in private." That's when I realized salvation is personal. Even if I had a marriage license, I had to walk this path with God on my own.

Ironically, the relationship itself felt better than the actual marriage. I once told myself I would never get married again—but I am not the Author and Finisher of my faith. God, who holds that power, clearly has different plans for me than I have for myself.

Missionary already told me: the plan I have for my life won't stand. God's plan will. I am His child, and His will shall be done in my life.

Wicked Spirits Raping Me in My Sleep

Since 2019, I have been tormented by wicked spirits attempting to rape me in my sleep. One of the most vivid and terrifying encounters occurred on the night of February 14, 2020. I had been plagued by intense homosexual thoughts, and in desperation, I decided to take communion. I asked my ex to send me a video that night for comfort, but she was reluctant. Eventually, she sent a video of herself in lingerie that I had not bought for her, leading me to believe she had other intentions for that evening. I ended up masturbating to ease the mental torment I was experiencing.

Later, I contacted a lady who agreed to take communion with me. After taking it, I felt a strange change in my body. Instead of comfort, I was gripped by fear and believed I was condemned. Since that night, I've refused to celebrate Valentine's Day. The Spirit brought this event back to my remembrance after I got married.

At one point, I received a prophecy that God would bless me and Tashoy with a baby. I cried out to God, questioning His righteousness. I told Him I didn't want to have a child with her after all that had happened, and I doubted whether He loved me. I thought He loved her instead, which pushed me deeper into hopelessness. Looking back now, I understand that God is righteous, and He eventually brought me out of that darkness.

While I was in a ward in Atlanta, I had another horrifying experience where a spirit raped me in my sleep. I was overwhelmed with anger and confusion. Throughout the rest of that year, similar assaults continued. I would wake up to find semen in my underwear, despite remaining celibate and fasting often. I cried out to God, asking why these things were happening to me.

Even after moving to Jamaica, the spiritual attacks persisted. One morning, I woke up with a burning sensation in my penis, and urination was extremely painful. I knew it wasn't a sexually transmitted infection because I had not been sexually active since arriving.

Stranger in Christ

To protect myself from these attacks, I developed a spiritual warfare routine. I began sleeping with my Bible open beside me, anointing my head, genitals, and feet with olive oil, and speaking specific Psalms over myself before bed. I also found that sleeping on my back reduced the chances of being assaulted. Whenever I felt a presence trying to overpower me in my sleep, I would call on the name of Jesus and rebuke it.

Of all the attacks from the enemy, these are the ones I hate the most. The enemy seeks to defile, to make me envy Christ, to blaspheme His name, and to give in to despair. I have told God that if He ever gives me the power to destroy the enemy, I would wipe them out in an instant.

Until then, I will continue to bring awareness to how real spiritual warfare is and how deeply witchcraft can impact someone's life. I am thankful that God is my healer, and if these are the trials I must endure for Christ's sake, I will bear them until He returns. With His strength, I will continue to build the kingdom of light and demolish the kingdom of darkness.

Wicked Spirits Tempting Me

I have experienced terrifying thoughts suggesting that I should curse God. Great fear gripped me when these ideas came into my mind. I often questioned how I could entertain such thoughts, especially knowing how much God has revealed to me. One night, a thought slipped out of my mouth—that I didn't like God—and I felt utterly defeated by that moment of weakness.

The torment didn't stop there. Thoughts like "I'm a woman trapped in a man's body" began to plague me. I was horrified. I told myself I'd rather die than give in to those temptations. There were times when I'd talk to men, and my body would react against my will. Because of this, I avoided looking men in the eye, especially during my job as a security officer. When couples approached, I would purposely look at the women to avoid the torment.

Despite all of this, I never acted on those thoughts. I never approached a man or expressed any of these struggles aloud. Writing this now brings me a sense of relief. I thank God that I've never crossed that line.

Temptation also came in the form of incestuous thoughts toward my siblings and male cousins. Whenever these thoughts surfaced, I would stop everything I was doing and remove myself from the situation. At times, I was even tempted to commit acts of violence, like harming my grandfather or cousin, or even burning down a gas station.

The enemy has tried every angle to pull me into darkness. But I have remained vigilant. I continue to call on the name of Jesus, rebuke the enemy, and stand firm in my faith. These experiences have taught me the importance of spiritual discipline, the power of prayer, and the need to stay grounded in the Word of God. Through it all, God has kept me, and I know that He will continue to keep me until the end.

Witches and Wizards in the Workplace

One evening while I was at work at FedEx, I clocked in and was immediately approached by a man who began speaking to me in a demonic tongue. Fear crept over me, as I wasn't sure whether I was about to be physically or spiritually attacked. I prayed right there and asked God to protect His son. I took note of the man's face and stayed alert for the rest of my shift.

On another night at that same FedEx facility, God told me to speak with a young woman. As I tried to approach her, I sensed resistance—as if spiritual forces were actively detaining her to prevent that interaction. The experience confirmed to me that I was walking in spiritual warfare, even at work.

Stranger in Christ

Later that year, I worked at the Walmart Distribution Center. One of the managers, in front of the rest of the leadership team, boldly told me that I should sign my name in blood. I was shocked and disgusted by such a blatant and offensive suggestion. I am a child of God, not of the devil. I prayed immediately, and the Holy Spirit told me not to worry—that He would deal with the situation. He reminded me that He would ensure no blood would be on my hands.

While working at AdventHealth, I became aware that one of the charge nurses was a witch. At first, I would participate in the food gatherings and celebrations on the unit. But as the Spirit began revealing more to me about the nature of some of my coworkers, I stopped eating at those events. Instead, I started buying my own food from the café.

One day, the staff was being treated by a doctor, and that same charge nurse asked me what I wanted. I politely told her I had brought my lunch and didn't need anything. She persisted, saying the food was free and I should accept it. I kept refusing. When she realized I wouldn't give in, she finally retreated. Strangely, toward the end of her time at the hospital, I began to smell a foul odor around her whenever she was nearby. I took it as a spiritual sign.

In all these environments, the Spirit of God has shown me that there are witches and wizards operating openly in many places. But He has also shown me that His protection surrounds me—even in hostile territory. These experiences have sharpened my discernment and reminded me that God is always with me.

Meditation

Meditation has become one of the most powerful tools in my walk with Christ. It gives me space to reflect on God's goodness and express my gratitude for all that He's done in my life. Scripture encourages us to keep our minds stayed on Him and to guard our hearts against the temptations and distractions of the world—including lust, pride, and worldly desires.

There's something holy about sitting quietly, away from the noise of technology and conversation, and simply listening for God's voice. His still, small voice brings comfort, clarity, and sometimes correction. I remember a time when I couldn't hear His voice, and it left me feeling confused. I wondered why God would show me visions but not speak directly to explain them. That silence drove me deeper into seeking Him.

Now, I've reached a place where I can close my eyes, enter into stillness, and hear Him speak—often before I even fall asleep. His presence settles me. He speaks to me through thoughts, memories, scriptures, and subtle impressions that bring peace to my soul.

The Spirit also led me to begin using social media for ministry. He specifically told me to start making videos on TikTok. At first, I was excited but unsure whether to speak in English or Patios. Eventually, I realized that English would help me reach a wider audience, so that's the direction I'm going. Being in Jamaica has boosted my confidence— being surrounded by family and people of my own culture has helped me speak with more clarity and boldness.

Before I record a video, I meditate on what God wants me to say. Then I find a quiet space with a peaceful background and begin to share. It's a blessing when I can speak without having to redo anything. I've also been planning to start uploading Bible studies on YouTube—something that's been on my heart for a long time. I didn't feel ready before, but the Spirit recently told me that I'm mature enough in the Word to teach it.

I've come a long way—from being a spiritual baby on milk to now being able to digest meat. The process of growth has been painful, but I thank God for His Word and for the Spirit who has comforted and shaped me for His purpose. Just like He told Jeremiah, "Before I formed you in the womb, I knew you," I know that He knew me too—and has called me by name.

God has even given me a new name. I tried to change my legal name, but was told I needed my wife's permission. Now that I've started the divorce process, I plan to finish what God started—changing my name to reflect the transformation He's done in my life.

Wisdom Entering My Heart

While working at the hospital, I discovered something extraordinary: my mind began to minister to me. It was like the Spirit was using my own thoughts to comfort me. My mind started creating songs—melodies and lyrics that glorified God. I was amazed by how intricate and meaningful the lyrics were, filled with wisdom and scripture. It reminded me of how fearfully and wonderfully made we are as God's creation.

Not only did my mind create songs, but I also began writing proverbs—short sayings that sounded like they came straight out of the Bible. I would post them on my WhatsApp status, and people were moved by the depth and insight in those words. I knew then that God was speaking through me.

After one of my fasts while living in Conyers, Georgia, I was blessed with the sweetest sleep I've ever had. I felt something being released into my spirit, and I descended into rest like I never had before. It was a reminder that the Lord gives sleep to His beloved. That peaceful sleep was a gift, a taste of the heavenly pleasures that are at His right hand.

One day at school, I noticed something white in my hair. I tried to pull it out, thinking it was something foreign, but it wouldn't come out. I soon realized it was a grey hair. I found more in my beard, and even on one of my legs. I was fascinated—not troubled. The elders I did Bible study with told me that God was trying to show me something.

The Spirit confirmed it: the grey hair was a blessing—a sign that wisdom had entered my heart. I've even had a vision where my entire head was full of grey hair. I look forward to the day that vision becomes a reality, because it will be a reminder that God's wisdom is growing in me.

Dreams About People's Deaths

I have received many dreams about people dying—some of them connected to my father's life and circle. One of the dreams that struck me deeply was about my dad's business partner. In the dream, I was standing in front of the restaurant, and he was looking for me. When he saw me, he began to hide, almost as if he was ashamed or afraid. Suddenly, a bolt of lightning struck him, splitting his body in two and burning his remains.

In another dream, I saw Chef's girlfriend, Marsha, die from a gunshot wound. The vision was intense and realistic, as though I had been physically present. I also had a dream about my dad's friend and barber, Squidly. In the dream, he too was shot and killed, though the specific details of how it happened were unclear.

What these dreams have in common is that they often involve people close to my father or involved in his business dealings. In yet another dream, a family member was calling and asking me about my father's whereabouts, as if they were urgently trying to find him. These dreams feel like spiritual warnings—not just about death, but about consequences, unresolved issues, and divine judgment.

I don't take these dreams lightly. When I wake up, I pray over them and ask the Holy Spirit for understanding. Sometimes, I am given clarity, and other times, I simply place the dreams at the feet of Jesus and ask for His will to be done. Whether literal or symbolic, I know that God uses dreams to reveal things that are hidden, and I remain open to whatever He wants to show me through them.

My Addiction to Porn

I was exposed to porn at an early age, but I didn't start watching it regularly until I moved to the United States. When I was living with my aunt Lisa, I would watch it on the computer and relieve myself in the process. One day while watching, I saw a dark shadow and heard a voice call my name— "TJ." I didn't answer, but I've often wondered who was calling me. Thinking back now, I believe it was my guardian angel trying to steer me away from that destructive path.

My aunt eventually found out what I had been watching on the computer. She confronted me, and when it came down to me, she gave me a beating. I told her I was going to hit her back, and she told me to go ahead. That was the first time I crossed a line with her—as she would say, I "passed my place."

Stranger in Christ

As I began to get sick, I realized that watching porn made my spiritual warfare worse. I believe it opened the door for demonic transfer from what I was watching. I rarely had sexual encounters as a young man, so I used porn as an outlet for my fleshly desires. But over time, I saw the harm it was causing me and cried out to the Lord for deliverance—and He delivered me.

At one point, my phone was full of pornographic videos, mostly from certain WhatsApp groups I was a member of. As I began to walk in my deliverance, I removed myself from those groups. The Lord told me it is not good for a man to be alone, so while I wait for Him to restore me and bless me with a Godly marriage, I try to resist sexual urges by staying busy or reading the Word. Sometimes I give in, but I remind myself—I'm still in the flesh, and I'm a work in progress. I do not frustrate the grace of God.

Fasting and Prayer

The Scriptures tell us that there are certain spirits we can only cast out through fasting and prayer. I remember the first time I fasted—I was sick, and the adversary didn't want me to do it. He attacked my thoughts, and I became scared because of the ungodly thoughts I was having. But it's because of prayer and fasting that I've reached the spiritual heights I'm at today. God has been taking me from glory to glory. He allows me to eat the fat of the land and enjoy the fruit of my labor.

Pastor Williams taught me about Isaiah 58 and how it applies to our lives. Now, whenever I fast, I use that scripture alongside Matthew 6:16–18. Through fasting, the Lord has renewed me from within. When people look at me, they can't tell I'm going through spiritual warfare or that I've been diagnosed with mental illness. Even psychiatrists and nurse practitioners have told me that I don't exhibit the mannerisms associated with my diagnoses. But I don't come into agreement with those labels.

First, I was diagnosed with acute psychosis, then bipolar disorder, followed by schizophrenia, and most recently, OCD. I told my family I don't have any mental issues, and I refuse to make those declarations over my life. I refuse to take the medications because they slow me down and make me feel like a zombie. They make my heart race, increase my blood sugar and blood pressure, blur my vision, cause rapid weight gain, and make my breathing shallow, among other things.

After spending my life trying to eat healthily, it didn't sit right with me to be forced to take pills they say I have to take for the rest of my life. I view both the diagnoses and my family's demand that I take those pills just to be around them as crimes against my spirit—so I separated myself from that side of the family.

Through fasting, God has given me revelations about my family. He's provided me with instructions concerning them, and I've even witnessed Him heal patients while I worked in the hospital. I know the power of fasting, and I've made it my mission to share this knowledge not only with my family but with anyone willing to listen.

A lot of people ask why I don't become a minister or preach from a pulpit. I tell them that taking care of the sick, the poor, the needy, the fatherless, and the widows is my portion of the Gospel. James 1:27 says, "Pure religion and undefiled before God and the Father is this: to visit the fatherless and widows in their affliction, and to keep himself unspotted from the world."

I've seen hospital patients who had been there for weeks, longing to be discharged but unable to because of their blood levels. After I spoke with them about the Lord and gave them scriptures to read and pray over, they were discharged soon after. I've cared for COVID patients and even forgotten to wear a mask a few times, but I've never gotten sick since I began working at the hospital.

My director once asked me to train a new CNA who had just started. She was studying to be a nurse and said she applied for the job because of me. I prayed and asked God not to let the person who trained me become jealous, and that the other CNAs who had been there longer wouldn't feel envious of the blessings God was pouring out on my life.

Stranger in Christ

One morning, a young woman came to the floor with her instructor to assist the CNAs. When I introduced myself and told her my name, her entire face lit up like the sun. She was so happy to meet me. It turned out I had cared for one of her grandparents, and they had spoken highly of the care I provided. She told me, "When my grandparents found out I wanted to become a nurse, they said they want me to be as good as you."

This young lady was white and had just graduated high school. She was heading to nursing school. Now, race has nothing to do with it—God is the Savior of all men. But it was the love I received from my patients, moments like this, that kept me going, even while I was battling my own illness.

Psalm 103:1–6 says:

"Bless the LORD, O my soul: and all that is within me, bless his holy name.
Bless the LORD, O my soul, and forget not all his benefits:
Who forgiveth all thine iniquities; who healeth all thy diseases;
Who redeemeth thy life from destruction;
Who crowneth thee with lovingkindness and tender mercies;
Who satisfieth thy mouth with good things; so that thy

youth is renewed like the eagle's.
The LORD executeth righteousness and judgment for all
that are oppressed."

One day, while breaking a fast, I went to a Jamaican restaurant in Atlanta to grab something to eat. When I walked in, the cashier looked familiar. After taking a closer look, I realized it was my cousin—from my mother's side of the family. We were both shocked and excited to see each other.

She asked me what I wanted to order. If my memory serves me right, I think I ordered soup to break my fast. She told me she was living nearby and working at the restaurant. I explained that I had recently moved to the area with my wife at the time. We exchanged numbers and stayed in brief contact. I had hoped we could hang out, but life took some unexpected turns, and it never happened.

Now, two years later, I'm staying with her grandmother—my aunt—in Hanover. I heard that my cousin is now married, has received her Green Card, and is going back to school to become a doctor. It's nobody but the grace of God working in both of our lives.

Jobs

I worked as a security guard for several years while I was attending university. I used to travel all the way to Miami for school. Eventually, I was promoted to supervisor at the security company. Although it was an honor, the position only came with a $1 raise. Around that time, my brother—an elder in Christ—told me he knew someone looking for a bus driver at an assisted living facility. I told him I was interested, and after an interview, I got the job.

After some time, I began cross-training to be a concierge, and eventually, I became the assistant to the business office manager. Then I got COVID and had to take time off work. When I returned, they had already given the position to the girl who had it before me.

After that, I moved to Georgia and met a man named Audley who worked at Toyota Stonecrest. When Nicole put me out,

Audley said he had a friend working at the Walmart Distribution Center and offered to help me get a job there. He tried to reach out to his friend Mark, but we couldn't connect him, so I applied on my own and got hired. I loved the job, and I even helped my uncle John get hired there as well.

It was the highest-paying job I'd ever had. I was truly grateful and thanked God every chance I got. Eventually, I resigned because the Holy Spirit told me to go to Jamaica. I went with the intention of being a dispatcher for my dad and Chunny's husband at the time, but that didn't work out, so I had to put those plans on the back burner. I spent five months in Jamaica—my longest stay since moving to the States. I spent a lot of time in nature, and God brought significant healing into my life. After a hospitalization, my aunt offered to bring me back to the States so I could get back on my feet. At first, I said no, but the Spirit told me to go.

Back in the States, I started working at Walmart again, though the hours were few, especially with school. My aunt spoke to a friend of hers, a director at the hospital, about hiring me as a CNA. I wasn't sure if I'd get the job due to my class schedule, but one day, I received an offer letter in my email. I accepted it immediately—especially since my aunt had just bought me a van and I needed better income.

That job turned out to be the best I've ever had. I take no credit for it. All the glory goes to God.

How to Eat

Christ says that we are the salt of the earth—and salt is good. Many are misled into thinking salt is bad, but it gives our food flavor and has benefits when used properly. The salt we should use is iodized sea salt. It helps reset the electrical activity in our bodies, and you can start feeling a difference once you begin ingesting it.

We're also told that wine is bad, and some believe it's a sin to drink it. I learned in Bible study that honey can be ingested with milk. I tried it, and it became a spiritual cleanse for me. After I started drinking milk sweetened with honey, my body began to react when I ate something that didn't agree with me.

The best oil to cook with is olive oil—it's considered holy oil. It doesn't contain trans fats or the high levels of saturated fats found in common oils. Other healthy alternatives include coconut oil and avocado oil.

To bind a wound, the Word tells us to use oil and wine, as mentioned in Luke 10:34. I've also found that after eating and drinking juice, it's beneficial to drink a cup of water. It helps with digestion and nutrient absorption in the stomach and intestines.

My elder in Christ, Clive, introduced me to ancient Japanese warm water therapy. You heat the water until it steams but don't let it boil. Drink it plain—no additives. It helps release gas from your body by making you belch or pass gas. After drinking it, wait at least 45 minutes before eating. If you exceed that time, it may cause bloating, but overall, it resets bodily functions.

This method improved my vision, helped regulate blood pressure and blood sugar, made my urine clearer, and improved my bowel movements. It worked wonders for me and for others I've shared it with.

Improved Health

I made a conscious decision not to take the medications that were prescribed for my diagnosis. Instead, I chose to depend on fasting and prayer. Through this, God improved my memory, restored my energy, and helped me lose the weight I had gained from the pills. I began waking up with morning wood again and going to bed with night wood every night. My ejaculations became thick, rich, and plentiful. But each time I resumed the medication, all of that stopped.

The Word says it's an abomination for a man who is wounded in his stones to stand in the congregation of the Lord. I refuse to take anything that kills my natural function. I reject those pills and will stand on that decision for the rest of my life.

At the start of the semester, I was hitting the gym, but then I stopped. Still, I found other ways to stay active. I started doing push-ups at home and walking laps around the lake—two to three in the morning on my days off and another two to three in the evenings. That helped keep the weight off.

My family started to comment on how healthy I looked and how well I was taking care of myself. I did all of that on my own—not with the help of a woman, but with the help of the Lord.

Cleanliness

While working at the hospital, I discovered how beneficial it is to shower both in the morning and at night. I would start my day with a warm shower to wake up and refresh myself, and after a long twelve-hour shift on the hospital floor, I'd take a cool shower in the evening to help my body relax and cool down.

About a year ago, I stopped using deodorants. Instead, I began using colognes, and I haven't looked back since. Unlike deodorants, colognes don't irritate my skin, and my underarms no longer develop odor after a while like they used to. My coworkers even started calling me the "Cologne King" because I always smelled good.

Patients often noticed too. Many of them would compliment my scent and speak highly to the nurses about my work ethic and personal hygiene. Some patients even told me I would make a great husband for their daughters. I'd humbly respond that I was already married.

One of my aunt's coworkers once told her that I was handsome and hardworking—and said she wanted me to marry her relative. Compliments like that reminded me that people notice the little things, and that good hygiene and a strong work ethic truly leave a lasting impression.

War

I once had a dream that Russia and China would invade America. In the dream, I was in an internment camp that was being run by those nations. The average American walks in arrogance, believing they are invincible—that they can't be touched. But I beg to differ.

The Word of God is truth and cannot lie, and it is in that Word that I place my hope and trust. According to the book of Isaiah, America is Mystery Babylon, the nation that seduces the whole earth. Like every great kingdom before it, it will eventually come to an end.

While I was in the psychiatric ward in Atlanta, God prophesied through the people there, declaring that I am in His army and that I am a son of David. When I heard that title, I said to myself, *That's the name of Christ they're calling me by.* I may not know what rank I hold in the Lord's army, but I am grateful that He found me worthy to be part of it.

As a soldier of the Lord, I searched the Old Testament for His commandments concerning warfare and the armed forces of Israel. I studied the Law, the book of Joshua, Judges, Samuel, Kings, and Chronicles—even the Apocrypha. If it involves spiritual war, you'll find me there. That's why I face so much spiritual warfare in my own life.

Battling a mind that fights against itself and making a comeback from that kind of darkness takes incredible perseverance. So, I continue to ask God for the strength to keep fighting—especially when the battle gets tough.

You don't have to go under the water to be born again

Conclusion

Solomon, the son of David, says in the book of Ecclesiastes that we should remember our Creator in the days of our youth, so that when the evil days come, it will be well with us. I have followed this instruction, and the Spirit has guaranteed me that He will never leave me nor forsake me.

I hold this promise close to my heart, especially as I face the fiery trials that have come to test my faith and the vision God has shown me for my life. I intend to remain steadfast in the Word, continuing to bear my cross so that I may be filled with joy and gladness at the second coming of Christ—and not be ashamed.

I've prayed to be a light for those walking in darkness, to live a Spirit-filled life, and for the Lord to order my steps and direct my path. Because I am strong in the Lord and on fire for the Kingdom, I desire to share my journey with young believers—and even those still in the world—to teach them how to fight in the Spirit. I want them to be built up and ignited with passion for the Kingdom of Christ and of God.

When Christ was on earth, His ministry was centered around healing. Since He has brought my soul back from destruction, I want to spend the rest of my life healing others through the Word and teaching them how to walk victoriously with the Lord.

Freely I have received—and freely will I give, just as the Word commands.

About the Author

The author is a dedicated follower of Christ whose journey has been characterised by significant spiritual growth, perseverance through challenges, and a passion for ministry. From early struggles with addiction, spiritual warfare, and mental health issues, they have undergone profound deliverance and healing through prayer, fasting, and the Word of God.

Their faith has been strengthened through meditation, Scripture, and a personal encounter with God's voice—guidance that continues to direct and sustain them. With a background in roles ranging from security supervisor to hospital CNA, the author sees their work as an extension of their ministry: caring for the sick and needy as a living expression of pure religion.

Driven by a passion for holistic healing, the author shares spiritual insights and practical wisdom regarding the benefits of fasting, prayer, and health practices inspired by Scripture and ancient therapies. Their ministry also extends onto digital platforms like TikTok and YouTube, where they inspire and educate a broad audience through Bible studies and messages of hope.

Stranger in Christ

Transformed not only in spirit but also in lifestyle, the author embraces clean living, healthy habits, and a rejection of harmful medications. Their life is guided by visions, dreams, and prophetic words, affirming their calling as a soldier in God's army—one who battles spiritual darkness with perseverance and faith.

Inspired by Christ's healing ministry, the author is dedicated to helping others overcome their struggles and walk victoriously in the Spirit. Their mission is to freely give the grace and wisdom they have received, igniting a passion for the Kingdom of God in both believers and seekers.

www.ingramcontent.com/pod-product-compliance
Lightning Source LLC
Chambersburg PA
CBHW061832040426
42447CB00012B/2939